W9-AVH-470

Traditions

Program Authors

Connie Juel, Ph.D.

Jeanne R. Paratore, Ed.D.

Deborah Simmons, Ph.D.

Sharon Vaughn, Ph.D.

PEARSON
Scott
Foresman

Glenview, Illinois
Boston, Massachusetts
Chandler, Arizona
Upper Saddle River, New Jersey

ISBN-13: 978-0-328-45279-8
ISBN-10: 0-328-45279-3

9 10 V011 14 13

CC1

Traditions

Sports 4

Why are sports important in our country?

The AMERICAN FLAG 36

What does our flag mean?

Contents

Sports

See page 35 for My New Words!

SPO

Run! Jump! Hit! Pass! Kick! Look at these kids playing sports.

Kids can play sports with teams. Baseball and football are team sports. Kids on teams work together. Team sports are fun!

Kids can play sports on their own too.
Track and bowling are sports that kids do not
need teams to play. These sports are fun too!

Baseball and football are sports that need two teams for a game. Look at these kids playing football. They bought special clothes and helmets that will help keep them safe.

The team in black has the ball. One kid throws the football. One kid catches it and runs with it. The team scores! They have won! Both teams will give high fives and say, "Good game!"

Track is a sport that kids can do on their own. At track meets, some kids run. Other kids jump. Kids may need to buy special clothes that make it easy for them to run and jump.

Look at this girl in red. She runs fast and then jumps as far as she can. She jumps three times. Her best jump will count as her score. Her worst jump will not count at all. This girl is good at jumping. It took her a long time to get this good.

Kids bowl one at a time. Kids drop the bowling ball and watch it spin down the wooden lane. They want the ball to knock down these ten white pins. The kids keep track of how many pins fall.

Some kids like to play team sports. Other kids like to play sports on their own. But many kids like both! Which sports do you like best?

Play Ball!

by Rita Lorenzo

Smack! Batters hit baseballs and run fast around the bases. Runners catch footballs and run fast to the goal. In many games, players kick, throw, spin, or catch balls. Can you name other sports that use balls?

Balls come in all shapes, sizes, and colors. Lots of balls are round, but balls can have other shapes too.

Look at all these balls. This boy likes to buy balls. He has won balls in contests too. He is a ball collector!

Look at these shiny new baseballs. Each ball is white and perfect. Perfect baseballs help pitchers throw well and help batters hit well.

When baseballs are made, an inspector checks each ball. It might be lumpy or have a funny shape. The worst balls get sent back. New baseballs are white with perfect stitches.

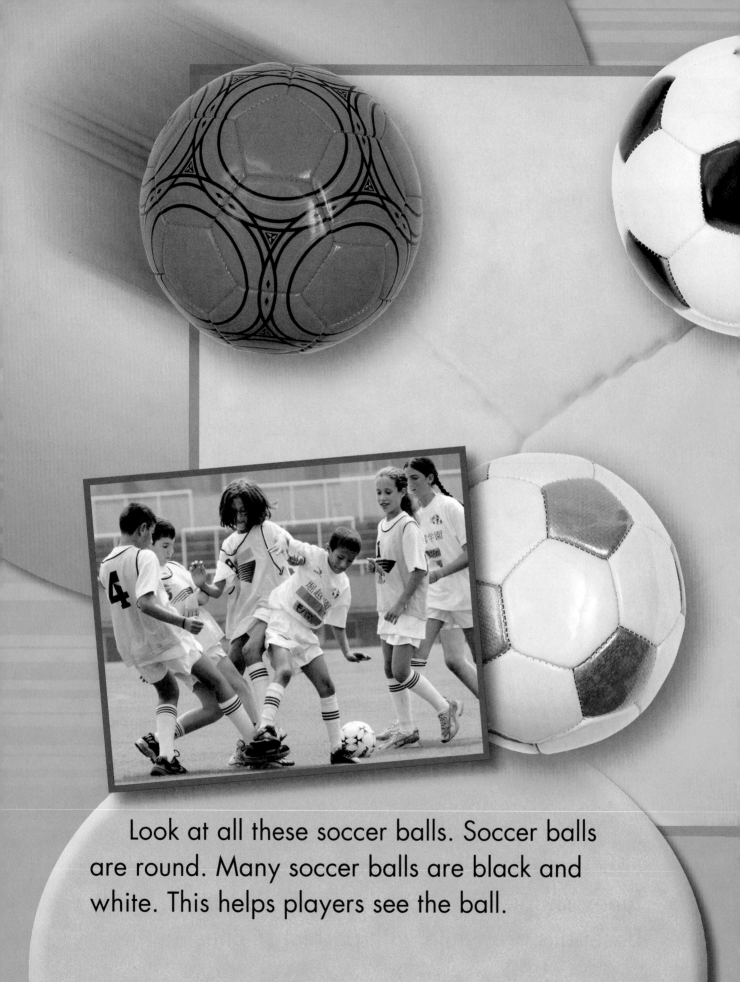

Look at all these soccer balls. Soccer balls are round. Many soccer balls are black and white. This helps players see the ball.

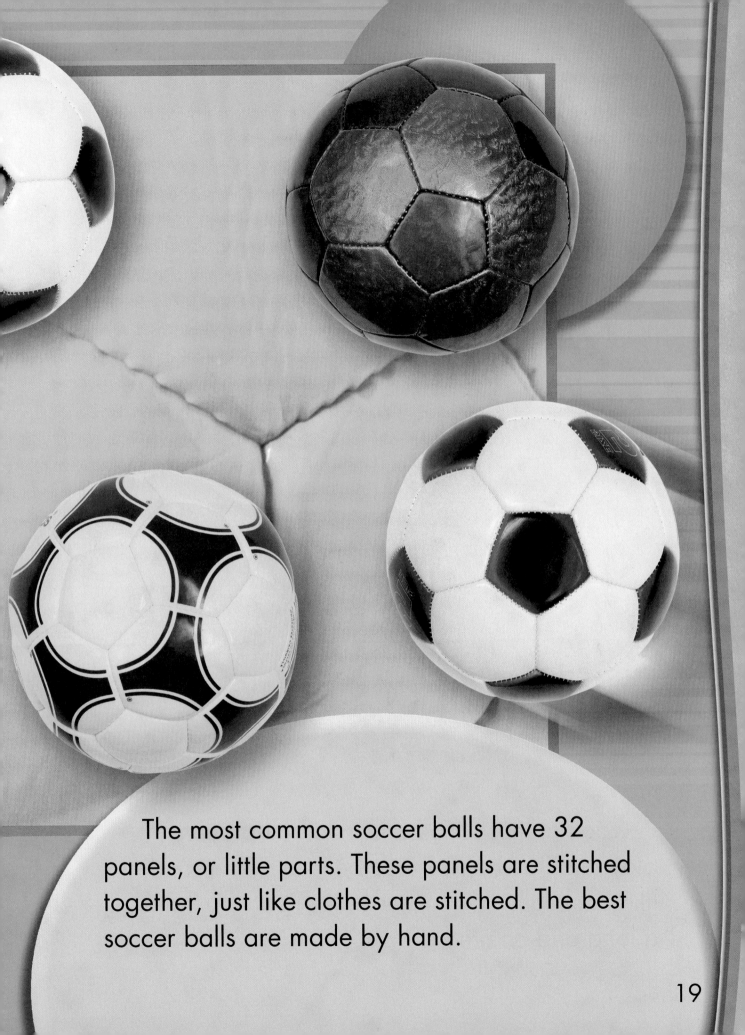

The most common soccer balls have 32 panels, or little parts. These panels are stitched together, just like clothes are stitched. The best soccer balls are made by hand.

Look at these footballs. Football players play with footballs. These balls are not round like baseballs and soccer balls. Footballs have a long and pointed shape.

If you had bought a football long ago, it would have been shaped like a watermelon. Today the shape now makes it easier for passers, runners, and kickers to throw, catch, and kick.

Now you know about baseballs, soccer balls, and footballs. Do you want to play ball?

THAT'S a Football?

by Thad Dorwood
illustrated by Mark Stephens

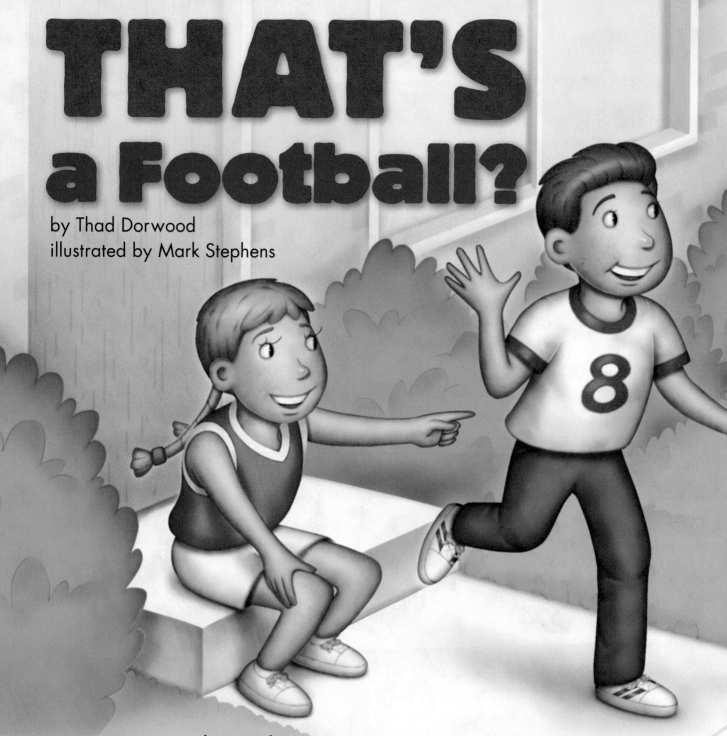

Tom and Brook sat on Tom's porch. "Look! It's Ken," pointed Brook. Tom and Brook stood up and waved.

"Look," beamed Ken. "I just bought this!"

"A football!" grinned Tom.

"Let's play!" smiled Ken.

22

"But we need one more player," said Brook.
Just then the kids spotted Ismail. He was a visitor from another country.

Tom piped up, "Ismail might want to play football with us."

"Ismail!" called Brook. "Ken just got this football. We want to play, but we need one more player. Will you play football with us?"

Ismail took the ball and shook it. "This isn't a football!" he cried. "How can you play football with this?"

Ken, Tom, and Brook looked puzzled. "What do you mean it isn't a football?" asked Ken.

Ismail took a ball from his bag. "In my country, this is a football," he said. His ball was round, black, and white.

"We call that a soccer ball," said Ken, pointing to Ismail's ball. "We call this a football."

"I don't know how to play football with that ball," sighed Ismail. "That ball is not round. How can you kick it?"

"We'll show you how to play football with this ball," grinned Brook.

Ismail watched them play. "You can pass this ball with your hands?" he asked. "When I play football, players can't place their hands on the ball."

"This football game is not like soccer. We can use our hands to pass the ball," added Ken.

"Players kick the ball like this," Brook chimed in. She showed Ismail how to kick.

"Do you want to play now?" Brook asked.
"I will be the worst player," groaned Ismail.
"Try it! I know you can do it!" smiled Brook.

Ken and Tom played on one team, and Brook and Ismail played on the other team. These kids ran and played for so long that their clothes got all dirty.

On the last play of the game, Brook passed the football to Ismail. He ran with it and made it to the goal line. Ismail scored!

"We won the game! Ismail is a football champ!" shouted Brook.

Ismail just smiled.

"Do you like this football game?" asked Tom.
"Yes, I like it a lot!" smiled Ismail. "It's fun!"
"Now let's play Ismail's football game!" cried
Ken. "I'll bet Ismail is a good player."

Brook grinned, "I'm playing on Ismail's team again! Ismail will be a football star no matter which football he uses!"

"Let's play," smiled Ismail. "But first tell me where you got your football. I want to buy one too!"

Get Ready to Play
Ice Hockey!

What are the parts of this uniform?
Why do you think a hockey player needs
each of these things?

helmet

face mask

shoulder pads

gloves

jersey

breezers

ice skates

My New Words

bought* She **bought** a new coat.

buy* When you **buy** something, you get it by paying money for it.

clothes* **Clothes** are things you wear on your body.

inspector An **inspector** inspects, or examines, something carefully.

stitch To **stitch** is to sew or fasten something with thread.

won* Their team **won** the game.

worst* Something that is the **worst** is as bad as it can be.

*tested high-frequency words

35

Contents

The American Flag

See page 65 for My New Words!

The AMERICAN FLAG

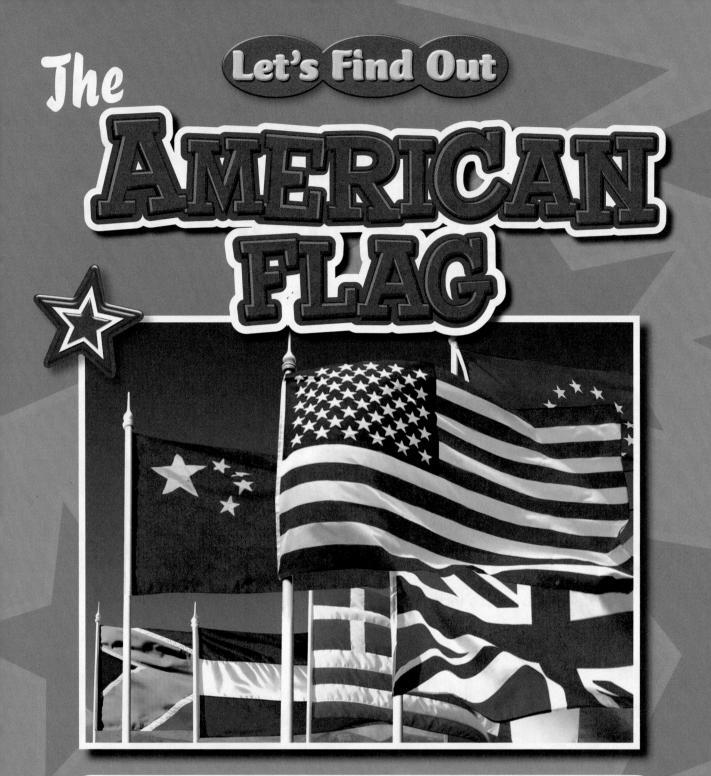

Did you know that every country has a flag? A flag can tell us a lot of things. A flag can tell us about that country's land and its people.

See that flag flying in the air. This is the flag for America. Our flag tells about our country. Here we are free to speak, think, and act. Our flag shows the world our pride in our homeland.

Our flag has six white stripes and seven red stripes. These thirteen stripes stand for our first thirteen colonies. Our flag has fifty white stars that sit on a blue background. Each star on our flag stands for a state.

Our first flag had thirteen stars because we started with thirteen colonies. As our country grew, the number of stars on our flag grew too. One star has been added for each new state. Our flag has had fifty stars for a long time.

Our flag flies in lots of places. Look outside. Is our flag flying on a flagpole at your school? Look in your town. You might see our flag flying outside your city hall or on firehouses.

But you will not see the U.S. flag flying just outside. You will see it in lots of other places too. Look on a letter before you mail it. Is our flag on the stamp? If you went to the moon, you would even see our flag flying there. It's true!

Whether our flag is flying on Earth or on the moon, we in America are proud of our flag. We are proud of what it stands for. Many people think that our flag is beautiful with its stars and stripes, all red, white, and blue.

Walk down the street in your town. Look up and down. Look all around. How many flags do you see? Quite a few? Here's to the red, white, and blue!

Taking Care of Our Flag

by Katie Sharp

America's flag flies in places all around the world. It flies all over the Earth and even on the moon. Our flag shows our pride in this beautiful land.

We have a few rules that help us care for our flag. We must not disrespect our flag. That would be a disgrace. We must keep it looking new.

The flag can be flown outside from sunrise to sunset. We need to take the flag down every night. If we leave the flag out at night, we need to shine a bright light on it.

When hanging our flag on a pole, the blue part hangs at the top and closest to the pole. When hanging our flag on a wall, the blue part is at the top and to the left. Our flag is never to be hung any other way.

We need to keep our flag clean and looking new. We must try to keep our flag in the air and off the ground. If our flag hits the ground, we need to clean it as soon as we can.

When a flag gets dirty, tattered, or ripped, we need to stop using it. The proper way to get rid of a flag is to burn it. This is a way to show respect for the flag.

We cannot use our flag as clothes. Those who care about our flag dislike this. It is fine to place a flag patch or pin on a coat or shirt. This does not show disrespect for our flag.

At pregame shows for many sports, the flag is hanging. We sing a special song about the flag and our country. Do you know this song? Can you sing it?

Broad Stripes and Bright Stars

by Lewis Clapham
illustrated by Joel Spector

"It's time to get up!" Dad called.
"It's Flag Day!" Mom added. "We do not want to be late for the Flag Day party! It is fun to be in Washington, D.C., for Flag Day!"

Josh and Drew dressed in red, white, and blue. They were in a city far from home. They flew here to see buildings and landmarks in this city. Many of these places are known all over the world. They are special to the people of America.

Mom had picked up maps.

"Let's read our maps so that we do not get lost,"
Mom stated. "I dislike getting lost!"

"It looks like the party is over there," Dad pointed.

When they got to the party, actors greeted them. The actors were dressed as if they lived in America's past.

Drew and Josh made flags with glue and precut red, white, and blue paper.

Then an actor called out, "It's time to meet the man who wrote a song about our flag—Francis Scott Key."

An actor dressed as Francis Scott Key stood up. He said he had seen America's flag flying over a fort after a hard battle in 1814.

"I was shocked that it was still waving in the air," he said. "I wrote about how this sight made me feel. Later, my writing was set to a beautiful tune."

"Let's stand up and sing my song about the flag!" he called.

Josh and Drew knew his song. "We sing this song at pregame shows at ballgames," Josh grinned.

Drew nodded. He had sung it with his class. This is America's song!

Drew did not want to show disrespect. He placed his right hand on his chest.
Josh, Drew, Mom, and Dad all sang.

"The flag that Francis Scott Key saw is still around. It is in that room," Dad pointed. "Let's go look!"

Mom, Dad, Josh, and Drew looked through glass windows and saw this old flag.

Workers were taking care of this flag to help it last a long time.

"It looks tattered and discolored," Drew noted, "but it is still the flag on this Earth that I like best!"

Old Glory

by Grandpa Tucker

Sing to the tune of
"On Top of Old Smokey"

I cheer for Old Glory
Each time it goes by!
And I love when I see it,
As it waves in the sky.

It stands for our country
And says we are free.
I'll always remember
It is special for me.

My New Words

air* The **air** is what we breathe.

America* **America** means the United States.

beautiful* If something is **beautiful**, it is very pretty to see or hear.

colony **Colonies** were places in America before it became a country.

Earth* **Earth** is the planet we live on. The **earth** is also the ground.

landmark A **landmark** is a place that is important or interesting.

respect The children show great **respect** for their parents.

world* The **world** is the Earth and everything on it.

*tested high-frequency words

Contents

Family Celebrations

See page 97 for My New Words!

Family Celebrations

I've got a big family. We're all happy to share special days in our lives. We like to share birthdays, weddings, and other happy times.

I like my big family. It is nice when
everybody is at a party. It is loud, but it is fun.
We eat good food and play fun games!

Young and old, we all like birthdays. We believe that birthdays are special and fun. We like to give gifts that are just right. We try not to spend too much money. It's the thought that counts.

My mom bakes our birthday cakes. She
makes the best cakes! We sing the birthday
song as loudly as we can. We're happy to make
someone in our family feel special.

My family likes weddings too. We've just had a wedding for my older sister. It was a very special day for my sister and for our family.

My sister was a beautiful bride. Her dress was white and fluffy. She'd never looked happier in her life. That made the family happy too.

My family likes to let Mom and Dad know how special they are. We have special parties for Mother's Day and Father's Day.

We make cards for Mom and Dad. We bring gifts. We try to help in the house. We want Mom and Dad to feel special. They like the fuss that we make.

My family likes to invite company to our parties too. A big crowd makes us all happy. It makes our parties more fun. We're with our family and our friends.

My family is big. My family is fun.
We like to share birthdays, weddings, and
other happy times. I like my big family.

Angel Food Bakery

by Catherine Anderstic

Look at the cakes on this ledge. Steph is a baker. She made these cakes. She can make cakes for everybody.

Steph can make wedding cakes, birthday cakes, and cakes for moms and dads. She can make white cakes, fudge cakes, and even bright red cakes.

Those who need cakes phone Steph. She asks them what size cake they need. If they're inviting lots of company, it will need to be big!

What flavor cake and frosting do they like? Is this cake for a birthday? Is the birthday boy or girl really young?

When it's time to make each cake, Steph gets her bowls, cups, and spoons. She greases her cake pans.

Now Steph makes the cake batter. She adds things like butter, flour, and eggs. She beats the batter with her mixer until it's smooth.

Steph spoons the batter into the cake pans.
She keeps filling them until they're just about full.
She puts them in to bake and sets the timer.

When the timer rings, Steph sticks in a toothpick to help her judge whether the cakes are done. She sets the cakes on a ledge. They've got to cool.

When the cakes are cool, she pops them out of the pans. Now it's time for frosting!

Steph frosts cakes in two steps. First she puts on a thin layer of frosting. Then she puts on a thicker layer. She is careful to get frosting all the way to the edges.

Next, Steph adds toppings. Toppings make each cake special. Wedding cakes might be frosted white and topped with flowers. Birthday cakes might have fudge frosting topped with dots. Steph cuts out circles and places them on this cake.

Steph made this cake for a boy's birthday.
She phones his mom to say, "It's time to pick up
his cake!" She takes pictures of all her cakes for
her cake book.

The boy's mom picks up the cake. She brings money to pay Steph. She tells Steph, "I believe the birthday boy will like this cake!"

Twice as Nice

by Clay Clark • illustrated by Jana Christy

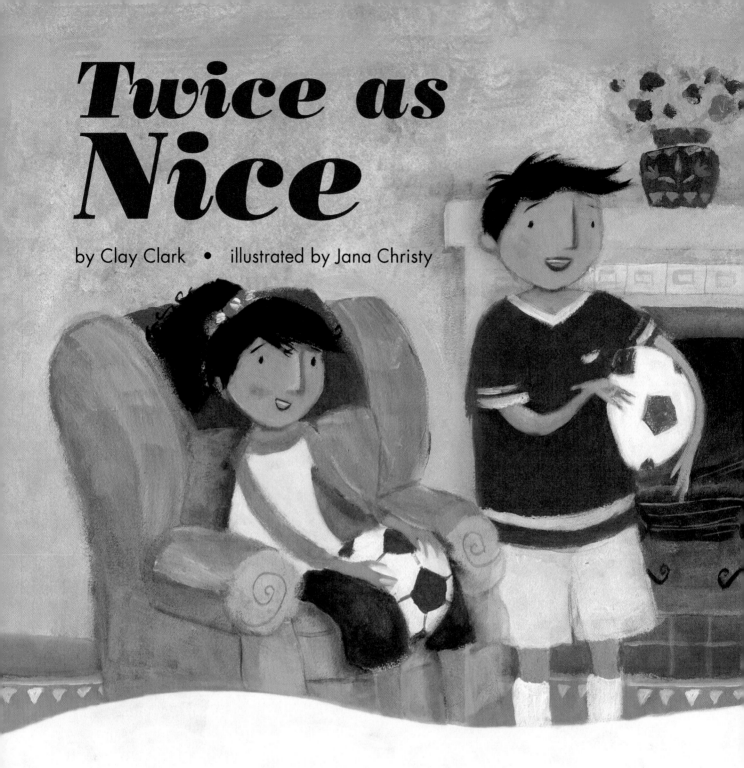

Midge and Phil are twins. They like doing things twice but never in the same way. If Midge spends her money on a red ball, Phil spends his on a blue one. Midge and Phil's birthday is next week.

They're planning what to do when they turn
nine. They both want their own party. But Mom tells
them they can have one big party.

"I will invite my pals to our party," smiles Midge.

"I will invite my pals," grins Phil.

Midge's pals phone. Then Phil's pals phone. They're all coming to the party. The young twins will have lots of company!

"We've got to make cake. What kind?"
Dad asks.

Midge pipes up, "I'd like fudge cake!"

"I'd like white cake!" Phil chimes in.

"I believe we'd better make them both!"
Mom smiles.

"What games will we play?" Mom asks.
Midge pipes up, "I'd like to play tag!"
"I'd like to play hide-and-seek!" Phil
chimes in.
"We'd better play them both," Mom grins.

In a few days, it is time for the twins'
birthday party. Pals bring gifts for Midge
and gifts for Phil. Mom places all these gifts
on a ledge.

After games, Mom gets the cakes from the fridge. Dad takes pictures as everybody sings "Happy Birthday" to Midge. Midge blows out all her candles. Then they sing "Happy Birthday" to Phil, and he blows out all his candles.

"Which cake would you like?" asks Mom. The twins and their pals giggle, "Both, please!"

Watch Where You Sit!

My New Words

believe*   If you **believe** something, you think that it is true.

company*   When you have **company**, you have guests.

everybody*   **Everybody** likes the new teacher.

money*   **Money** is the coins and paper used for buying and selling things.

young*   When something is **young**, it is in the early part of its life.

*tested high-frequency words

Contents

A Cowboy's Life

A Cowboy's Life

Giddap! It's fun playing cowboy. But do you know about real cowboys?

Cowboys did lots of work in the Old West. Some rounded up cattle that roamed the land. Others herded cattle on long trips between ranches and train stops.

Could a woman do this work too? Yes, there were some cowgirls in the past. But most helped run ranches instead.

Look at this cowboy from the past. The first thing you might notice is his big hat. The wide brim kept rain, snow, and sun off the cowboy's head and face.

cowboy hat

chaps

spurs

boots

The cowboy wore leather chaps over his pants. Chaps kept his legs safe from thorny shrubs and cactus plants. This cowboy also wore leather boots. Spurs on the heels helped prod his horse to go faster.

Cowboys spent lots of time riding horses. They sat in leather saddles with their boots in stirrups. They held onto leather straps that helped steer the horse.

Cowboys needed to know how to handle ropes. They knotted one end of a rope and made a loop at the other end. Cowboys used these ropes for jobs such as catching cows and dragging wood.

A cowboy's life was not easy. He spent lots of time alone. He worked outside, even in bad weather. A cowboy had to look out for rattlesnakes too! To pass time, cowboys liked singing songs.

Are there still cowboys? The answer to that question is yes! Cowboys still put on hats, chaps, and boots. They still ride horses and use ropes. They work at ranches and at horse shows.

Nat Love
A Great Cowboy

by Renata Graham   illustrated by Adam Gustavson

Nat Love was a well-known cowboy. He was good at riding horses, herding cattle, and using ropes.

Nat was born a slave in 1854. When he was seven, battles started between the states. When the fighting ended, slaves were given freedom. Nat got a job to help his family. He tamed wild horses so that cowboys could ride them.

When Nat was fifteen, he felt ready to live by himself. He headed West all alone.

Nat met cowboys in a town called Dodge City. He wanted to join them. These cowboys asked him questions. They wanted to know if Nat could ride untamed horses.

Nat got on a wild horse named Good Eye. It didn't take long for these cowboys to notice that Nat was surprisingly good at riding untamed horses. When Nat dismounted his horse, these cowboys gave him a job.

Nat rode with these cowboys for a long time. He learned how to use ropes to catch cows. Nat herded cattle between the cowboys' ranch and Dodge City.

When Nat was 22, he entered contests in a town called Deadwood. Nat had to ride horses and use ropes in these contests. Nat won easily and got a big prize. Big crowds clapped happily for Nat. News about Nat's skills spread all over the West.

Nat rode as a cowboy until 1889. Then ranchers no longer needed lots of cowboys for herding cattle. Nat took a railroad job. Around this time he met a nice woman. She and Nat had a wedding.

Nat wrote a book about his life. In it he tells tales of things he did and places he saw. We know from these tales and other people's stories that Nat Love was one of America's finest cowboys.

THE LIFE AND ADVENTURES OF NAT LOVE
BETTER KNOWN IN THE CATTLE COUNTRY AS
DEAD WOOD DICK
BY HIMSELF

Heather at the RODEO

by Maddy Tuxbury
illustrated by Rosario Valderrama

"Did you see that cowboy, Mom?" Heather cried. "He rode that bull for such a long time! He stayed on even as it twirled and twisted around the ring!"

"He's one brave cowboy!" Mom smiled.

"Bull riding is the riskiest contest at these shows," Dad added.

Dad looked like a cowboy himself. Heather giggled at the cowboy hat he wore on his head.

Dad said, "Let's go! It's time for barrel racing.
There isn't much time between these shows!"
    They rushed to the barrel-racing event. They
got there just in time.

Right away, Heather noticed that cowgirls were getting ready to race. She asked Dad questions about this.

"This race is just for cowgirls," Dad stated. "They ride horses around those three barrels. The fastest woman wins."

Heather held her breath as each cowgirl raced. "They ride so fast!" she cried.

Next, it was time for roping races. Mom explained roping to Heather.

"Long ago, cowboys used ropes to handle cattle. Now roping is part of these shows. Roping takes lots of skill for both cowboys and horses."

"Cowboys on horses rope young cows as fast as they can. The fastest team wins," added Dad.

Heather looked on as a young cow stood alone. A cowboy rode out on his horse. He twirled his rope over his head and tossed the loop onto the cow's head. Then he dismounted his horse and tied the young cow with his rope.

"Which show is next?" Heather asked.

"Riding horses without saddles is next," Dad replied. "In this contest, cowboys can grasp only one leather strap with one hand. They try to stay on their bucking horse for 8 counts."

Heather looked on as cowboys on unsaddled horses took turns riding. Each horse bucked up and down, up and down. Each time, Heather counted to 8 in her head. Some cowboys held on. Some rode unsteadily, and then fell off!

Mom, Dad, and Heather headed out. Heather told them that she wanted to be a cowgirl. She grabbed Dad's cowboy hat, placed it on her head, and yelled, "Giddap!" Then she trotted all the way to the car.

Did You Know?

Cowboys wear hats to protect their heads. Long ago, cowboys used hats as water bowls too.

Cowboy boots have pointed tips to help cowboys guide their feet into the stirrups.

Branding cattle with a mark to show who owns them began long ago in ancient Egypt.

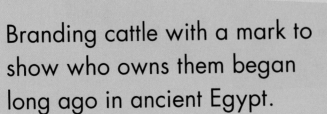

My New Words

alone* If you are **alone**, you don't have anyone with you.

barrel A **barrel** is a container with a round, flat top and bottom and sides that curve out a little bit.

between* There is a rock **between** the two trees.

buck My horse began to **buck**, but I managed to stay on.

bull A **bull** is the full-grown male of cattle.

notice* If you **notice** something, you see it.

question* A **question** is what you ask in order to find out something.

woman* A **woman** is a grown-up female person.

*tested high-frequency words

Contents

Celebrations for Everyone

See page 159 for My New Words!

Celebrations for Everyone

Sing! Eat! Throw a party!
Get the word out! It's time to have fun from dawn till night!

Kids and grown-ups all over the world celebrate special days. Let's find out how.

United States: Independence Day

130

In this place, it is taught that the new year starts with a new moon. Moms, dads, and kids celebrate for fifteen days. On the last day, people might dress up in red and lift lanterns. Some walk in long lines under a huge dragon.

China: New Year

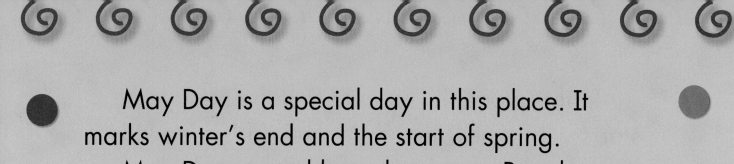

May Day is a special day in this place. It marks winter's end and the start of spring.

May Day started long, long ago. People felt happy because the cold days of winter had finally ended. Snow and ice had thawed, and it was time for spring.

England: May Day

People celebrate May Day with songs. Lots of kids gather around tall, skinny Maypoles stuck in lawns. These poles have long ties. Kids grab these ties and skip around the Maypole.

In this place, people throw big parties in streets. They put on fun masks and dress up in bright costumes. Lots of masks hide just half their faces.

Brazil: Carnival

At these big street parties, those who dress up might ride on big, fancy floats.

These parties can last for days and days. If kids miss a day of fun today, there will be more fun tomorrow!

In this place, kids and grown-ups celebrate crops. Before May, crops are planted. Then in August, people pick them. They come here from many miles away with yams and other crops.

Ghana: Homowo Festival

Pals and families get together. They eat lots of fish and cornmeal. Many people play drums. There is a special party for twins too. When all this celebrating is finished, people start planning next year's fun!

The Sweet Stink of Success

by Nick Horner

illustrated by Kevin Rechin

Do your sneakers stink? Does the dreadfully awful smell make Mom and Dad's skin crawl? Do pals pinch their noses each time you take them off? And do you just shrug at all this fuss?

If you've discovered that the awful stink is your sneaker's fault, there is a contest for you. It's for kids who think their stinky sneakers are bad enough to be good. They can enter the Rotten Sneaker Contest!

The Rotten Sneaker Contest takes place in March. Kids proudly show their smelliest, dirtiest, and most displeasing sneakers.

Being a contest judge is not easy. Half the time, judges want to plug their noses! Sneakers get judged on looks, as well as smell. Judges must check sneakers' soles, heels, and laces. Then they unhappily give each sneaker good, long whiffs.

Winners of the Rotten Sneaker Contest get nice prizes. Grand prize is cash that the winner must place in a bank. Prizes also include money for new sneakers, and inserts for keeping those new sneakers smelling sweet.

Finally, all winning stinky sneakers end up in the "Hall of Fumes." You'd need to have a cold to not smell these stinkers!

Being stinky can bring big prizes! But if you think winning is easy, get your nose checked! Contest winners say winning is hard. Some keep sneakers on day and night and even sleep in them!

Others rub their feet to make them sweat. And today's winners have these helpful words for kids wishing to be tomorrow's winners: Do not put on socks.

Do you have what it takes to stink?

Austin P. Crawler's Naughty Pig

by K.K. Sarna
illustrated by Alan Flinn

Austin P. Crawler had the naughtiest pig in Sauk County.

You might ask, "How can a pig be naughty?" The answer is: Austin's pig ate everything he saw. Don't you think that's a naughty thing to do?

Surprisingly, Austin's pig did not just sit in his straw bed all day and yawn. He did not grunt and snort in mud and muck.

No, this pig ate. He ate everything he saw.

147

He ate all the dinner scraps that the Crawler family fed him. He ate all the chickens' grain and all the horses' oats. The chickens and horses got scrawnier, and Austin's pig just got bigger.

This naughty pig ate rakes and blankets.
He ate plows and tractors. He ate nice, hot
wagons in the winter. He ate ice-cold mailboxes
in the summer.

One day the pig gobbled up half a windmill from the lawn! Didn't I tell you he was the naughtiest pig in Sauk County? He ate everything he saw.

I bet you'd like to know what Austin
did when his pig ate all this stuff. Well, he
didn't do a thing. He didn't even say a word.
You see, Austin P. Crawler had an
unexpectedly grand idea.

Tomorrow was the Sauk County Fair. And at this fair there would be a contest to see who had the biggest pig.

Everyone knew that Austin had the naughtiest pig in Sauk County. But more than that, Austin knew that he had the biggest pig too. And, hopefully, his pig would win.

The next day, Austin was up at dawn, feeding his pig. He fed him saddles. He fed him ladders. He fed him corncribs and flower pots.

And finally, Austin fed his naughty pig a few scraps from last night's dinner.

Then Austin P. Crawler led his pig to the fair. They got there just in time for the Big Pig Contest.

And that's when Austin saw a small girl hauling a huge trailer. What was in that trailer? Can you guess?

If you said a huge pig, you're right!
That day, Austin's pig didn't get a prize for
being the biggest pig in Sauk County.

But each pig in the Big Pig Contest did get a shiny, new ribbon. And Austin's pig ate them all. He ate everything he saw.

Austin P. Crawler's pig might not be the biggest pig in Sauk County. But he's still the naughtiest.

Piñata Game

Cinco de Mayo means May 5. That's when people of Mexico celebrate with parades, dancing, and games. They play this game.

- Hang the piñata.
- Blindfold the first player.
- Spin the player three times.
- Give the player a stick, and face the player toward the piñata.
- The player swings at the piñata three times.
- Repeat until someone cracks open the piñata. Treats will pour out for everyone to enjoy!

My New Words

cold*

Something **cold** is not hot. I can't come to school because I have a **cold**.

corncrib

A **corncrib** is a building or bin for storing corn.

county fair

A **county fair** is an outdoor show of farm animals and other things.

finally*

I **finally** figured it out.

fume

Fumes are gases or smoke that have a bad smell.

half*

A **half** is one of two equal parts.

tomorrow*

Tomorrow is the day after today.

word*

We speak **words** when we talk.

*tested high-frequency words

Acknowledgments

Text

Every effort has been made to locate the copyright owner of material reproduced in this component. Omissions brought to our attention will be corrected in subsequent editions. Grateful acknowledgment is made to the following for copyrighted material.

64 Margo J. Tucker *"Old Glory" by Bob Tucker from www.grandpatucker.com/sg-oldglory.html-ssi. Copyright © 1996–2000 by Grandpa Tucker's Rhymes and Tales and its licensors. All rights reserved. Used by permission.*

Illustrations

Cover: Rosario Valderrama; **22–32** Mark Stephens; **37, 64** Ruth Flanigan; **54–62** Joel Spector; **66, 68–77** Kathryn Mitter; **67, 88–95** Jana Christy; **96** Mick Reid; **98, 116–125** Rosario Valderrama; **108–115** Adam Gustavson; **129, 138–145** Kevin Rechin; **146–157** Alan Flinn.

Photographs

Every effort has been made to secure permission and provide appropriate credit for photographic material. The publisher deeply regrets any omission and pledges to correct errors called to its attention in subsequent editions.

Unless otherwise acknowledged, all photographs are the property of Pearson Education, Inc.

Photo locators denoted as follows: Top (T), Center (C), Bottom (B), Left (L), Right (R), Background (Bkgd)

Cover: (BL) ©John Henley/Corbis, (BR) ©photolibrary/Index Open, (TL) ©Royalty-Free/Corbis, (CR) Getty Images; **1** (CL) ©John Henley/Corbis; **2** (B) Getty Images; **3** (BR) ©Fritz Curzon/ArenaPAL/Topham/The Image Works, Inc., (T) Ike Scott/On Track Visual Communications; **5** (TCR) ©Michael Newman/PhotoEdit; **6** (Inset) ©Michael Newman/PhotoEdit, (C) ©William Sallaz/Duomo/Corbis; **7** (C) ©Bob Daemmrich/The Image Works, Inc., (CR) ©Tony Garcia/SuperStock; **8** (C) ©John Giustina/Getty Images; **9** (TL, CR) ©John Giustina/Getty Images; **10** (C) ©Rudi Von Briel/PhotoEdit; **11** (C) ©Tom Carter/PhotoEdit; **12** (C) ©Royalty-Free/Corbis; **13** (BR) ©Royalty-Free/Corbis, (C) Getty Images; **16** (BL) ©Cut and Deal Ltd/Index Open, (C) ©Kent Gilbert/AP/Wide World Photos; **17** (BR) ©John Russell/AP/Wide World Photos; **18** (BL) ©Issei Kato/Reuters/Corbis; **20** (C) ©Jim West/Alamy Images, (CL) Getty Images; **21** (C) ©Ariel Skelley/Corbis; **34** (C) ©William Sallaz/Corbis, (Bkgd) Design Pics, (TR) Getty Images; **36** (C) Getty Images; **37** (CR) ©William Manning/Corbis; **38** (C) Brand X Pictures; **39** (C) ©Royalty-Free/Corbis; **40** (C) Brand X Pictures; **41** (C) ©T.D.M. Co., Red Oak, IA/Library of Congress; **42** (C) ©Sal Maimone/SuperStock; **43** (C) NASA; **44** (C) ©Donald Nausbaum/Getty Images; **46** (C) ©altrendo images/Getty Images, (Bkgd) ©Royalty-Free/Corbis; **47** (BL) ©Mike King/Corbis, (T) ©Shaun Egan/Getty Images, (BR) ©Stephen Saks Photography/Alamy Images; **48** (Bkgd) ©Royalty-Free/Corbis, (C) ©William Manning/Corbis; **49** (CR) ©age fotostock/SuperStock, (T) ©Joseph Sohm; ChromoSohm Inc./Corbis; **50** (C, BL) ©Robert W. Ginn/PhotoEdit, (Bkgd) ©Royalty-Free/Corbis; **51** (C) ©B.S.P.I./Corbis; **52** (T) ©Gaetano/Corbis, (Bkgd) ©Royalty-Free/Corbis, (BC) GRIN/NASA; **53** (C) ©Sven Creutzman/Corbis; **67** (CR) Ike Scott/On Track Visual Communications; **78** (CR, CL) Ike Scott/On Track Visual Communications; **79** (TC, CR, CL) Ike Scott/On Track Visual Communications; **86** (BR, BL, BC) Ike Scott/On Track Visual Communications; **98** (L) ©Royalty-Free/Corbis; **99** (TR) ©Bettmann/Corbis, (BR) Getty Images; **100** (C) ©Bettmann/Corbis, (T) ©Emely/zefa/Corbis; **101** (C) ©Bill Manns/The Art Archive; **102** (C) ©Bettmann/Corbis, (C) ©Geoff Brightling/©DK Images; **103** (C) DK Images; **104** (C, Bkgd) John C. H. Grabill/Library of Congress; **105** (C) The Granger Collection, NY; **106** (C) ©Bettmann/Corbis, (T) ©Frank Lukasseck/Corbis; **107** (C) ©Royalty-Free/Corbis; **108** (C) Getty Images, (C) The Granger Collection, NY; **111** (R) Rare Books, Manuscript & Special Collections Library, Duke University; **114** (L) Rare Books, Manuscript & Special Collections Library, Duke University; **115** (BL) Rare Books, Manuscript & Special Collections Library, Duke University; **126** (BR) ©Geoff Brightling/©DK Images, (TR) ©Howard Sokol/Index Stock Imagery, (BL) Getty Images; **128** (BL) ©Krzysztof Dydynski/Lonely Planet Images, (C) JASON LEE/Reuters/Corbis; **129** (BR) ©Tony Freeman/PhotoEdit; **130** (BC) ©Joe Drivas/Getty Images, (BL) ©John Henley/Corbis; **131** (BR) ©Krzysztof Dydynski/Lonely Planet Images, (C) JASON LEE/Reuters/Corbis; **132** (C) ©Gideon Mendel/Corbis, (BL) ©Royalty-Free/Corbis; **134** (C) ©Iconotec/Alamy, (BL) ©Owen Franken/Corbis; **135** (BR) ©Jeff Greenberg/The Image Works, Inc.; **136** (BL) ©Fritz Curzon/ArenaPAL/Topham/The Image Works, Inc., (C) ©Christoph Henning/Das Fotoarchiv/Black Star/Alamy; **137** (BR) ©David Cleaves/Alamy; **158** (C) ©Tony Freeman/PhotoEdit.